THE BODY POLITIC

Maggie Jaffe

Attica Press

Grateful acknowledgement to the following journals in which many of
the poems first appeared:
*The Women's Review of Books; The Minnesota Review; Amnesty
International Anthology; Poets' Voices: 1984; San Fernando Poetry
Journal; Social Anarchism; Telegraphy; No Hay Fronteras!: Poems for
Peace in Central America.*

Cover design: *Atrocities Management: El Salvador* by Deborah Small.

Attica Press
Box 40122
San Diego, California 92104

*for Harold, compañero,
and for Shavootz, cat*

CONTENTS

IN THE DISTINGUISHED LIBERAL NEWSPAPER

I read of the Salvadoran poet
now living in Nicaragua
who came here to speak
of her country (Neruda's
"delicate waist of America")
of the rich volcanic earth
of *corona de cristo* that blooms
blood red
of executions in the dark /
dark cages of the dying
of "white hands" smeared
on their victim's walls.

The distinguished liberal
newspaper headlined its story
"Salvadoran Misery." Of course
severed heads are a misery.
Mutilated Indians are a misery.
Military escalations promoted
as humanitarian aid are a misery.

And yet *she* speaks of revolution
in San Salvadoran factories
in liberation churches
in pueblo-owned *milpas*
after monsoon when the sweet
green corn ripens.

(for Claribel Alegria)

LANGUAGE OF POETRY

A friend of a friend,
a "lyric" poet,
charged me with wanting
to change the world through
my poems. At the time I didn't
respond, not having formulated
an answer sound enough not to appear
glib. Both of us would concede
that words can describe the complex
inner life, love for animals,
names for trees both bare
or leaved, love for another human's
body, glowing under
tangled yellow sheets.

It's not enough.
Words also *Liquidate,*
Pacify, Terminate.
Orders given / received:
sever a limb, excise a nipple,
delete a government enemy.

From a Salvadoran prison
Roque Dalton wrote of the lyric
 poet 's surprise when smashed
against a prison wall.

After police knocked out his teeth
then hacked off his hands,
the poet-singer, Victor Jara,
led the Chilean people
in the soccer stadium in song:
Veñceremos.

And yet since Dalton, Jara: cruelty
institutionalized. What then can
poetry do?

"POVERTY SUCKS"

"We have the right
not to know about the poor,"
my student wrote
after I showed the class
photos of people working.
Specifically a Haitian cane-cutter,
propped up on his scythe, dead
asleep on his feet.

This particular cane-cutter
earns 5 *gourdes* for 10 hours
(approximately one dollar a day).
With luck he'll live to be 54:
in Haiti the sun is boss
and the bosses are boss.

My student vacations in the Bahamas,
sips his *Cuba Libre*,
eyes the girls, tans (the sun
his personalized bullion),
doesn't see the sweating Blacks.
Has never seen anyone sweat
at work: not on TV, not in videos,
not in movies.

I should give him no more than a "D"
(as in "dollars" "detonate" "dread"),
but he still wouldn't *get* it:
that a man can be so broke
he falls asleep on his feet.

DEATH OF CHE

On the day that
Che Guevara died
a woman, thirtyish,
from the wealthy
"first circle"
of La Paz,
exploded her
heart with a
snub-nosed .38.
Radios played
Morir por Amor:
to die for love.
Even his executioner,
Barrientos, that shit,
felt a "great loss"
at his dying.

                    Rain in the Sierras,
                    frost.
                    When it cleared:
                    crystalline.
                    Flowering cacti,
                    poppy, maize.
                    Che was betrayed
                    by the CIA
                    and Bolivian peasants
                    he meant to aid
                    wanted to love.

Che said:
"I can't sleep
on a mattress while
my soldiers are
shivering up there."
And he divided men
into two groups:
those who can sleep

on a mattress while
others suffer
and those who cannot.

TAPESTRY: MOTHERS OF THE DISAPPEARED

Who was Sebastian Acevedo?
Immolated himself in front of Concepcíon
Cathedral when he learned that his son
and daughter were being tortured.
To police he was a "Marxist
motherfucker," a "pro-Cuban agitator,"
according to the CIA.

Where were they tortured?
Cinema rooms: South Vietnam;
Production rooms: the Philippines;
Blue-lit Cabaret: Chile.

> **The promiscuity of Democracy**
> **is excessive.**

When the Sebastian Acevedo Movement
picketed the offices of *El Mercurio*,
the cops also arrested their
ten-foot cross, threw it in back
of an unmarked truck.
Can they make a wood cross talk?

Where's Pinochet? Holed up
with Los Chicago Boys, economists
who've studied with Milton Friedman.
Together they delivered the shock
treatment to Chile's flagging economy.
But the number of "subversive poor" have tripled:
the military equate poverty with Marxism.

In North America I teach Composition,
a kind of torture but not "torture."
In his youth Pinochet attended
the American School for Coups.
What did he learn?
        Electric Shock

Mock Execution
Operating Table
Parrot's Perch
Sexual Humiliation
Submarino
Telephono
Witnessing the Torture of Others.

> *We have found the solution*
> *for de-politicizing the universities:*
> *expel half the students*
> *expel half the professors*
> *cut the curriculum in half.*

Since the coup, *arpilleras*, a cottage industry, was developed: tapestries made into patchwork depictions of Chilean life. Working-class women create *arpilleras*, churches sell them abroad. One in particular shows miniature Mothers of the Disappeared who have chained themselves to the Santiago Police Academy fence. Over their hearts are photos of their loved ones--the women hold up a banner: *AQUI SE TORTURA* / HERE THEY TORTURE! Behind them are multicolored Andes and a smiling sun. The last figure is truncated, except for her arm, clenched into a diminutive, but unmistakable, upraised fist.

IN A SAN DIEGO SWEAT

shop
wedged between massage
and tattoo parlors
Chinese women sew
piece work.

At their bone-tired
feet, "camo" cloth
become uniforms--
become soldiers slain
on alien fields--
become money in the bank,
that you can bank on.

For luck & prosperity,
a red wax Buddha lights
up the shop's dark corner.

For lunch: rice with
shrimp speared on chop-
sticks, gaudy and plastic.

I think of red-crowned
cranes *(Grus antigona)*
hunched up in chemical waste.

VIGILANTE
> "Who was Bernhard Goetz,
> and why did he do it?"
> *Time*, April 1985

After shooting three Black
youths the "subway vigilante"
shoots the fourth again. ("You look
all right, here's another.")
The .38 severs his spine.
Goetz
will walk the streets
ride the subway
read the *Times*.

Now the newspapers want to know
who is Bernhard Goetz?
He is a computer
technocrat, your neighbor,
scared shitless, white.
And the shot boys,
who are they? Name-
less, indistinguishable,
out of work.

December 2nd, 1859,
madman, "vigilante,"
John Brown
hanged for opposing
slavery. Emerson wrote:
"He will make the gallows
holy as a cross."

Meanwhile, a hundred-
thousand-odd lynched Blacks
later . . . On a quiet suburban
street shots ring out
(fireworks? family squabble?).
We keep our children's

lights on after dark.
Their toys sprawled out
on the uniform lawns
like minuscule anti-
personnel mines.

EVERYTHING HAPPENS AT NIGHT
(In Memory, Steve Biko,
died September 12, 1977)

In South Africa
everything happens at night.
Night held captive, smeared,
retched
in Soweto, Nyanga, Sharpeville . . .
At railway stations, cinemas,
restaurants, toilets
("Non-Whites Only"),
color itself is void.

Copper sun, sere earth,
weaver bird song,
mealie fields at dusk.
In the veld, night
is lion-tongue,
giraffe-knowing,
antelope-grace
impressed on pale
gold Krugerrands.

Suburban swimming pools,
chained guard dogs, white
walls splashed with bougainvillea,
protea, cape primrose.
In Black townships only thorn
trees survive.

"When I'm nervous," she says,
"I have a double scotch
and clean my husband's rifle."
Outside, the Karoo *dorp*
bellows like a wounded wildebeest.
Waiting for what?
       Steve Biko, brain injury.
       Jacob Monakgotla, heart attack.

James Lenkoe, natural causes.
Dumisani Mbatha, unknown illness.
Joseph Mdluli, application of force to neck.
Lawrence Ndzanga, natural causes.
Neil Aggett, hanged himself.
Sifundile Matalasi, self-strangulation.
Thabo Mosala, internal bleeding.
"Looksmart" S. Ngudle, suicide by hanging.
J.B. Tubakwe, suicide by hanging.
Ahmed Timol, fell out of tenth story window.
Solomon Modipane, suicide by hanging.
Ernest Dipale, hanged himself . . .
"Official Version,"
yet their names snake
through unrecorded history
like the yellow
Molopo River.

In *shebeens* not enough
brandy to wash-
clean their dying
        not enough night—
Business as usual in the mines,
extricating gold and diamond
bullets: "Nigger rhymes with trigger"
in this suck, suck, suck hole
South Africa.

12 September 1984.
"South African police and Black
rioters battle in the township
of Soweto.
Killed: thirty-two.
Wounded: three hundred."
        Nyana we sizwe: brothers of the land,
        here is where you stand.
        There *is* witness.

BARTLEBY IN THE 19TH CENTURY

Our shadow.
Fissure on the blame-
less bullion sun.
No sun on Wall Street.
Between the courtyard,
blackamoor sky, the ceaseless
hunt, dollar-slaughter.

On Wall he scratches
out rich men's
mortgages, testaments
(for the poor
to say *I prefer not:*
a luxury: hollow
bones, memory,
a mouth).

Your sunset. Tall buildings
half-hid in shadow: canyons
on "endless" plains
where the spent
tribes weave history.
Winter. Passenger
pigeons ca-cooing
in a white elm
(Ulmus americana).
Along the Hudson, grass
is Flemish brown.

> *Melville at evening*
> *walks the ringing*
> *streets past the redskinned*
> *tenements, southeast*
> *from Gansevoort to Trinity,*
> *resurrectionless.*
> *Cobblestones pierce his feet,*
> *his mind a web*

                    of nuance.

Damn you, Bartleby,
there's money
to be made:
currency, bullion,
chattel to serve,
serve us.

THE NAMES

Catbird . . .
Her nest intricately woven
with grass, hair, plastic.
("For your poem," you smile).
Late July becoming August.
Already winter's signature:
crickets stridulate to husk.
Soon molting, now abundant chickadees,
nuthatches, bobolink (first sighting).
Incessantly, a rufous-sided towhee's
"drink your tea, drink your tea."

Rain-soaked hemlock, beech, white oak,
a country road. Our closest neighbors are
house wrens, family of four:
perpendicular tails, scolding mouths.
A catbird's *mew mew*
changed to hissing
when she sees us.
Her single nestling--deformed--
skitters through the rich growth:
born tail-less, defenseless
from child or hawk.

Where were we exactly?
Western Catskills--
"unpeopled" land settled
by the Dutch, later the English
who "huddled and built small."
Hunched against the elements, themselves,
they parceled out the wilderness.
The Indian didn't "waste" the land,
had no reciprocal claim to it.
Their names are a palimpsest, obscured
by concrete, dumping sites, testing grounds.
Name them shadows-of-extinction:
Oneida, Seneca, Onondaga, Cayuga, Mohawk.

What prairie-sickness trekked with them
across the dreadful Bering Strait?
Clearly color-obsession,
measured by the white
standard, gold or silver.

I read Ibuse's *Black Rain*
in "Indian country"—-
The sky is horribly blue,
from Hiroshima journals, August 10th.
Would we bear such light?
Years later an outpost in Danang
will be called "Fort Apache."
Still in Nam, a captain tastes
the viscous orange liquid to prove
to his men it's harmless.

That night Ursa Major
drags across the Mohawk trail.
Sky is milk. In the morning
I learn the names for wildflowers:
yarrow, pearly everlasting,
jewel weed, loose strife.
On the radio: "Imagine yourself
in the moist jungles of Borneo,"
called environmental sounds.
Without jungle, simulated jungle,
or "put yourself in a Cherokee wagon."

Clearing after rain,
so that sky is robin's egg blue.
The ice-cold pond fed by underground springs
takes our breath: we cry out like children.
In our murky mythic past,
our nightly romance,
our unlegislated nature,
Indians peformed daily rituals
of bathing en masse before dawn;
Europeans thought "perfume more rational."

A solitary catbird (*Dumetella carolinensis*),
joker, *heyoka,* most readily identified by its call,
"a downslurred, catlike *mew.*"
And still she hisses,
as if that nest would weave us sleep
or reason / reasoned sleep,
if only we remain here.

KANDINSKI IN EUROPE

"Blue melts to black"

Moscow, 1916, early winter.
Blue-black mottled clouds,
the Neva seized with ice.
From Izmaylovsky Park, faintly,
a Chopin mazurka,
while trains move
men westward to the front.

From a top floor flat on Dolgi Street
Kandinski reconstitutes the crowd
in the square
          as geometry: "point
to line to plane."

In anemic light he waits
for the future.
The samovar is piping hot,
windows coated with fine
traceries of frost.
In his corridor the smells
of potato, cabbage,
eau-de-cologne.
With each inhalation
his cigarette a diminutive amber
moon.

Years before Europe's Black Night,
Kristallnacht, he moves to
Weimar, Germany. At Bauhaus
their motto:
"creation equals the new society."
One step ahead of the goose-
stepping multitude, France
will be his final refuge.

O Germany—

hearing the speeches that ring from your house,
     one laughs.
But whoever knows you reaches for a knife.

HACKER
> *(for   Katya   Komisaruk,*
> *given 5 yrs)*

Not your Sixties
hippy-dippy anti-tech,
but a new breed:
whitemale, 25, computer
science major, suburban
mall shopper, church goer.

Can access anything:
NASA, Bank of America,
the Pentagon, the Vatican.
Will work for
IBM, TRW, UNISYS
(dreadful in South Africa).

Replicating, self-
destructing viruses
have been planted into
military computers.
According to *Time*
the culprits are "techno-nerds
with primitive social skills
and a startling indifference
to personal hygiene."
Your hacker does *not*, we repeat,
care a fig for peace.

POLICE / STATE

> U.S. Police training in Uruguay, *Hidden Terrors,*
> A. J. Langguth, 1978

He picks up the phone: oddly
his orders are *en Ingles:*
a grade "B" film
noir remembered
from a neighborhood cinema.

That they're so gringo
makes sense to you now,
having seen that photo--a "picnic"
in their south--their children
laughing, their women serving
coffee to the white-
hooded men.
Above them, the stiff
black body, swollen black
tongue.

He's gone. Now nothing
can be said. Sure, you'll
talk and live with that.
His crime? He wanted to kill
the hunger that is killing
us.
Now his assassin's
 President--made for TV--
with God's help, dollars
and police.

Here everyday objects are
catalysts of terror:

a chair strapped to,
a desk slammed on,
a phone hooked to genitals.
On *this* phone-as-instrument-of-torture
you note (in fine print)
"You have a friend at AT&T."

[In white rectangular rooms
in North America, poets
police their poems
deleting pointed references
to what is done in their names.
And yours.]

NOTES

"Death of Che": The quoted stanza is adapted from "Prayer For The Dead," Fina Garcia Marruz, *In Cuba*, by Ernesto Cardenal (New York: New Directions, 1974).

"Tapestry: Mothers of the Disappeared": The italicized text is adapted from "Proclamations Issued by the Chilean Military Junta," *Latin American Revolutionary Poetry*, ed. by Robert Marquez (New York: Monthly Review Press, 1974).

"Kandinski in Europe": The italicized text is adapted from "Germany," Bertolt Brecht, 1934.

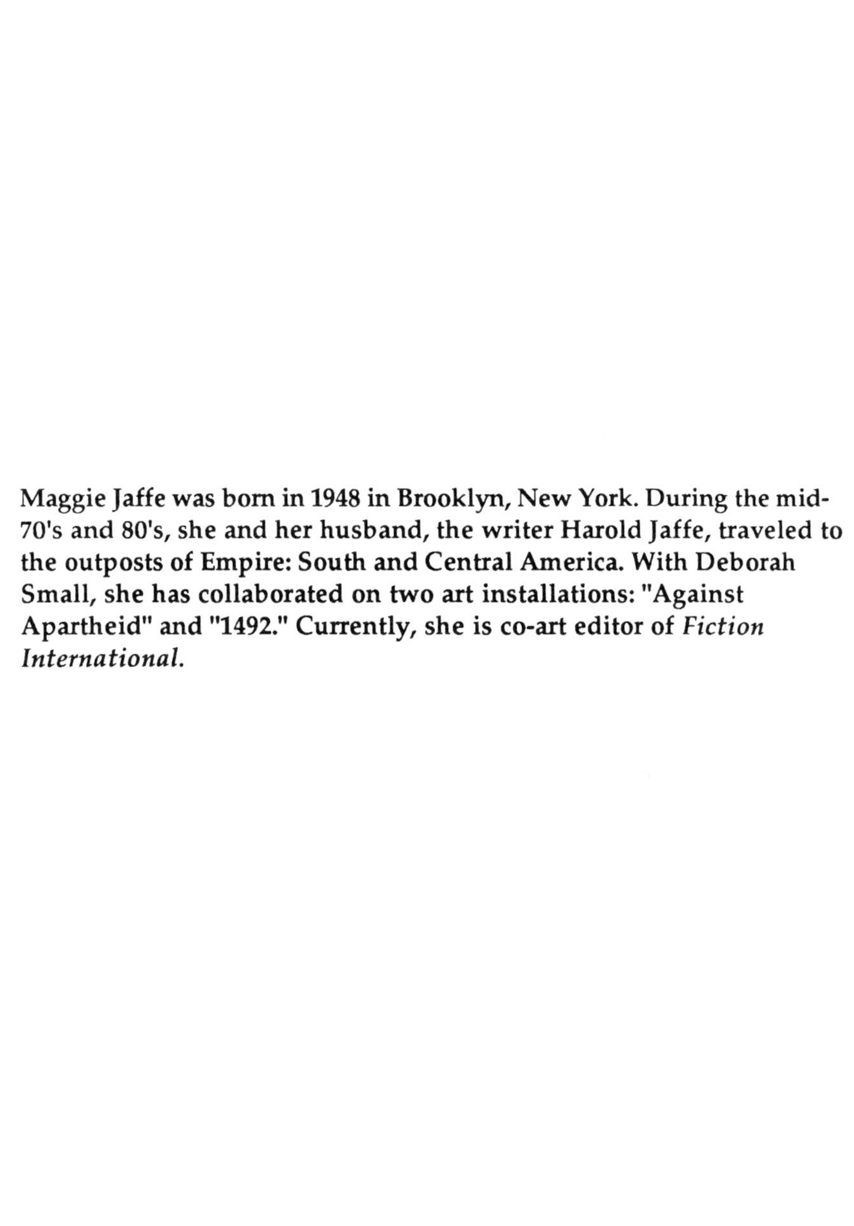

Maggie Jaffe was born in 1948 in Brooklyn, New York. During the mid-70's and 80's, she and her husband, the writer Harold Jaffe, traveled to the outposts of Empire: South and Central America. With Deborah Small, she has collaborated on two art installations: "Against Apartheid" and "1492." Currently, she is co-art editor of *Fiction International*.